Final Story Obituary Planner

Plan ahead for peace of mind

ManeLock Communications

Printed in the United States of America
Copyright © ManeLock Communications (The Writing Doula)
Text by Linda Jones
Design by Zachary Jenkins
Book cover by Sharon Jones-Scaife

ISBN-13: 978-0-9741645-1-9

Welcome to Your Final Story Obituary Planner

Your Final Story Obituary Planner is a handy guide to help you prepare your own obituary. By following this guide, you can leave your loved ones a thoughtful gift that will also be very useful when the time comes for them to honor your memory and acknowledge your life.

You will also be documenting your personal history for generations to come.

Your planner provides step-by-step instructions for creating a personalized obituary that will make it easier for a loved one to step in and complete the final version. Your planner package also provides tips on writing a less traditional version of your Final Story – if you wish to leave your loved ones a more personal legacy.

Your Final Story Obituary Planner includes customized fill-in forms to help you organize your personal information. The forms, once completed, will be a handy and important resource when you are ready to write.

Write your Final Story – then get on with your life!

Table of Contents

*"Obituary writing is more about life than death:
the last word, a testament
to a human contribution."*

The New York Times

Writing Your Standard Format Obituary

Step 1 – Fill in the Life Summary and Family Summary forms

Completing these forms will help you collect the information you will need to begin writing your obituary. The **Life Summary** forms list essential personal information, including your birthdate, birthplace, education, employment and other pertinent life events, achievements and interests. The **Family Summary** forms will help you gather names of immediate family and special friends you wish to be included in your obituary. Fill out both sets of forms completely. To assure accuracy, check with family and friends to be sure names are spelled correctly and to verify any other information.

You should update these forms periodically as your personal information and family situations change. Save the completed forms to your computer, cloud file or on a USB disk. Print copies for yourself and give copies to trusted family members for safekeeping until needed.

Step 2 – Write the obituary announcement

A standard format obituary traditionally opens with an announcement that a person has died. It gives the deceased person's full name and other facts, including his or her profession, family status (single, married or divorced), and military experience if applicable. The opening paragraph also prominently lists the city and state where the deceased lived. Some families include the cause of death in the opening paragraph, others prefer not to.

Since you are writing a draft of your obituary, you will set up this paragraph with "cue words" so that whoever completes the obituary on your behalf will know where to fill in the pertinent information. When writing this paragraph, you should refer to yourself in the third person.

Here is an example of how to set up the opening paragraph with cue words:

> *Frank Williams, a grocery store manager, devoted family man and longtime resident of Cleveland, Ohio, died (Date), (Cause of death). He was (Age).*

Here is an example of an opening paragraph with the cue words replaced by actual details:

> *Frank Williams, a grocery store manager, devoted family man and longtime resident of Cleveland, Ohio, died March 3, after a long illness. He was 58 years old.*

Step 3 – Write your brief biography

The second part of a standard obituary is a brief biography that includes the deceased's birthdate, birthplace, and a sampling of other information about their life. You will be able to write this section without having to leave space for any cue words, but whoever writes the final version of your obituary may want to add personal comments from people who were close to you.

The biography section could look something like this:

> *Frank was born on September 7, 1953 in Pittsburgh, Pennsylvania, the oldest of six children born to Donald and Mabel Williams. Frank lived in Pittsburgh until 1971 when he graduated from South High School and moved to Cleveland to attend college. Frank graduated from Arbor College in 1975, with a bachelor's degree in business. He went to work at Big Food Market and in less than a year was promoted to store manager. Frank loved his job and worked there for 30 years before retiring in 2005. Frank met his wife Regina (Jackson) during his freshman year at Arbor College and married her a month after they graduated. During their 35-year marriage, they had four children. Frank was a deacon at St. John CME church and was a longtime volunteer at the Cleveland Boys' Club. "Frank treated me like his son, even though he had four kids of his own," said Roger Johnson, who met Frank through the Boys Club. "Even when I left the program, he never stopped treating me like family."*

Step 4 – Acknowledge loved ones

This section is where mistakes are common — especially if family information is not readily available. Refer to your completed **Family Summary** forms to make sure that everyone you want to mention is recognized. This section may need to be updated periodically as family situations change through births, deaths, divorce, etc.

Family members typically included in standard obituaries are:
* Spouse or partner
* Parents (including mother's maiden name)
* Siblings and their spouses
* Children, stepchildren and their spouses
* Grandchildren, great-grandchildren (by count, not name)

~Listing in-laws: Spouses of the children of the deceased are typically named in parentheses next to the name of the person they are married to. The same goes for the siblings' spouses.

~Listing grandchildren: Grandchildren and great-grandchildren are typically recognized by a number amount and not by name to cut down on length of the obituary – the longer the obituary, the more it costs to publish. If you aren't sure of the number of grandchildren, play it safe and write "many" or "several" grandchildren.

~Listing deceased: Close family members who 'preceded' or died before you, can be mentioned in the acknowledgments first (i.e. Frank was preceded in death by his parents Donald and Mabel Williams).

~Places of residence: List city, state, and in some cases, country, next to each name.

A sample acknowledgement section:

Frank was preceded in death by his parents Donald and Mabel Williams. Remaining are his loving wife, Regina Jackson Williams, sons, Terry (Beverly), Mark and Frank Jr. (Sophie) of Miami, Florida; daughters, Gloria Parks of Detroit, Michigan, and Irene Morgan of Miami; brother, Gregory Williams of Detroit; six grandchildren; best friend Yolanda Brown of Baltimore, Maryland; and his beloved pet dog, Shepherd.

Step 5 – Bereavement information

People who will want to pay respects at your funeral count on obituaries to provide details about the funeral arrangements and related bereavement information. The information on the following check-list is typically included at the end of the obituary. Most of this section will be completed by whoever steps in and writes the final version of the obituary on your behalf, but you may want to make note of any special requests (i.e. donations to charitable organizations).

Be sure to include:

- Date, time and location of the wake or visitation
- Date, time and location of funeral or memorial service
- Burial information
- Repast information
- Name of funeral home or crematory handling the arrangements.
- Include your special requests (i.e. where to send charitable donations, etc.)

Here is sample bereavement information:

Visitation will take place Thursday, Sept. 7, from 6 p.m. to 9 p.m. at New Tabernacle AME Church, 243 Snyder St., Cleveland, Ohio. The funeral will be at the church on Friday at 11 a.m. Interment will be at Grace Memorial Cemetery, 1234 Connor Avenue, immediately after the services. Hughes Funeral Home is handling the arrangements. The family asks that donations be made to the American Cancer Society in lieu of flowers.

Step 6 – Write your complete obituary draft

Write a full draft of your obituary as instructed in Steps 2 through 4. Review and make any adjustments or corrections. Save a copy of your draft to your personal computer, cloud file or USB disk. Make a printout for yourself and provide copies to someone you trust for safekeeping and future use.

When you are done, congratulate yourself for leaving your loved ones a thoughtful legacy!

Date_____

Write the obituary announcement. (See Step 2)

Write your brief biography. (See Step 3)

Write acknowledgments of loved ones. (See Step 4)

Write bereavement checklist and instructions. (See Step 5)

My Obituary Draft

Date_____

Final Story Essay

My Final Story Essay Tips

At the appropriate time, one of your survivors will have to step in and complete your self-written obituary. But a Final Story essay is something you can write completely on your own.

A Final Story essay is not a death announcement, but a reflection on your life. Also known as 'autobituaries', they have become a growing trend by many who want to leave a more personal  legacy for their loved ones. Final Story essays are not intended to replace the standard format obituaries that are commonly used in publications and funeral programs, but they are usually written as a more reflective addition to them.

There is no rule that says your Final Story essay must be somber or sad. It can be humorous and entertaining. You can share tender and funny memories, leave sage advice, tell stories or share life lessons. You might even want to write how you would like to be remembered.

Even though self-written obituaries allow more freedom of expression, it is always a good practice to be accurate and responsible with what you write. Keep that in mind as you create final stories that will become a part of history and perhaps a cherished legacy for future generations.

On the next pages you will have space to write your own Final Story.

My Final Story

Date_____

My Final Story

Date_____

Date_____

This form, when completed, will be a valuable resource when it is time to write the obituary draft and the final copy. Fill in the blanks as completely as possible. Doublecheck the spelling and other facts to make sure they are correct. Update this form periodically as situations change.

Your name

Birthdate

Birthplace

Spouse/Partner

Number of children

High school

Other schools attended

Occupation/profession

Military status

Religious or spiritual affiliation

Place of worship

Hobbies

Accomplishments (degrees, awards, experiences, certifications, etc.)

The information in this section will be filled in by the person who steps in to complete your obituary.

Date of death

Age of deceased

Date, time, location of funeral/memorial service

Burial information

Repast information

Comments from friends or family about character of the deceased (Optional).

Date_____

Family & Special Friends of

Mother

Father

City/State

(Other guardian or caregiver if applies)

City/State

Spouse/Life Partner Name & Relationship

City/State

Offspring

List names of offspring, their relationship to you (i.e. son, daughter, etc.) their city, state and names of spouses if applicable. Note: For space considerations, grandchildren are acknowledged by total number instead of by individual names. Also, if you plan to acknowledge relatives who are already deceased, indicate by writing "deceased" in parenthesis next to their names on the form.

Number of sons

Name

Spouse

City/State

Name

Spouse

City/State

Name

Spouse

City/State

Name

Spouse

City/State

Name

Spouse

City/State

Name

Spouse

City/State

Name

Spouse

City/State

(Copy this form if you need more space.)

23

Number of daughters

Name

Spouse

City/State

Name

Spouse

City/State

Name

Spouse

City/State

Name

Spouse

City/State

Name

Spouse

City/State

Name

Spouse

City/State

Name

Spouse

City/State

(Copy this form if you need more space.)

Number of stepchildren

Name

Spouse

City/State

Name

Spouse

City/State

Name

Spouse

City/State

(Copy this form if you need more space.)

Number of grandchildren

Note: Grandchildren are rarely listed by individual names but by the total number.
Siblings
Number of Brothers

Name

Spouse

City/State

Name

Spouse

City/State

Name

Spouse

City/State

Name

Spouse

City/State

Name

Spouse

City/State

Name

Spouse

City/State

Name

Spouse

City/State

(Copy this form if you need more space.)

28

Total sisters

Name

Spouse

City/State

Name

Spouse

City/State

Name

Spouse

City/State

Name

Spouse

City/State

Name

Spouse

City/State

Name

Spouse

City/State

Name

Spouse

City/State

(Copy this form if you need more space.)

30

List any other relatives, friends or pets that should be included in the obituary if space permits.

Name #1

Relationship

Spouse

City/State

Name #2

Relationship

Spouse

City/State

Notes

Order additional copies

Encourage your family and friends to plan ahead by sending them copies of Final Story Obituary Planner. It is also a useful resource for counselors, church and spiritual organizations. For ordering information and group rates call us at: 214-803-3920 or visit: www.thewritingdoula.com/contact

Made in the USA
Columbia, SC
11 February 2020